Hockey Moms

Realities from the Rink

JULIE BERTUZZI

FENN

M & S

Library and Archives Canada Cataloguing in Publication
is available upon request

ISBN: 978-0-7710-1350-8
e-book ISBN: 978-0-7710-1351-5

Published simultaneously in the United States of America by
Fenn/McClelland & Stewart, a division of Random House of
Canada Limited, a Penguin Random House Company

Library of Congress Control Number is available upon request

Typeset in Electra by M&S, Toronto
Printed and bound in the USA

Fenn/McClelland & Stewart,
a division of Random House of Canada Limited,
a Penguin Random House Company
www.penguinrandomhouse.ca

1 2 3 4 5   19 18 17 16 15

Penguin
Random
House

*Thank you to my husband and children
for being my inspiration. Not only for this book
but for my life. I live to love you guys more every day.*

Contents

Thanks, Mom

As I wrote this book, and thought about all the moms I label, tease, and poke fun at in its pages, in the back of my mind I was always aware of the person who had one of the greatest influences on me growing up. My Ringette Mom is the reason I'm the stellar woman I am today. The jury's still out on whether that's a good thing or a bad thing, but, either way, I am extremely blessed. And for you Hockey Moms who don't know what ringette is, I could try to explain the sport, but as soon as I said the words "cut-off hockey stick, no blade, and a rubber ring," you would just look confused. So Google it!

Throughout the many seasons I played ringette, at tournament time my mom packed up our chocolate-brown, wood-panelled station wagon – you all know the one: the long, ugly, rectangular beast with the back seats that faced the cars tailgating you. (Seriously frightening when I think about it now.) She had that wagon jammed with helmets, pads, sticks, a ghetto blaster, and everything else we needed. She always gave a lift to any kids and moms who couldn't afford the gas to drive to the rink themselves; she always offered to pay for dinners that someone couldn't pay for; and she always ploughed through sleet, snow, rain, and hail to get us to our games. Not once did I ever get in the wagon to go home and get yelled at for playing a crappy game. She was the most positive influence in my life and in my husband's life, and she continues to be one in our children's lives as well.

My mom is a two-time cancer survivor and the toughest, sweetest lady I know. Often when I'm sitting in the stands and I erupt into an episode (or two) of "Hockey Mom crazy," I think of her. At games, she simply sits, watches, and cheers on her grandkids, just happy to be there appreciating the moments. She inspires me to look at my kids' games in the context of the big picture. While I'm no Oprah, I am wise enough to reflect on what's important in life, and that is to take the time to enjoy every game, practice, tournament, and weekend that we have to share with our kids. Embrace them, cheer for them, and hug them, even after a bad game (maybe *especially* after a bad game). We all may be a little nuts – or a lot nuts – when we get into the rink, but at the end of the day we have to be our kids' biggest fans. My mom was mine, and now I'm hers. I don't scream obscenities at her or tell her she sucks at vacuuming, but I do expect her to keep on being the best bad-ass, choir-singing, church-going mom ever.

Mom, I love you and thank you.

Before We Get Into It

Hi ladies!

Are you a Hockey Mom? Well, let's get real here, ladies: if you've picked up this book, the answer to that question is probably "yes." But do you know which kind of Hockey Mom you are?

In this funny little book, you will meet several types of Hockey Moms that exist in our arenas today. Twenty of them, to be exact. While we moms all have perceptions of our kids' personalities on the ice, it may come as a surprise to learn that we also have habits and ways of showing how *we* operate. Whether it's how we display our deep affection for referees, coaches, and the parents on opposing teams, or how we respond to the big plays on the ice, or even how we interact with our fellow Hockey Moms, we are all one type or another – sometimes more than one – of the Hockey Moms described in the pages of this book.

Before we get too far into it, let me tell you why I am qualified to write this book. First off, I am seriously guilty of being numerous sorts of Hockey Moms. Second, I am the wife of NHLer Todd Bertuzzi. We met when we were both seventeen – as some might say, we were high-school sweethearts. More accurately, I would say we were OHL sweethearts. We spent as much time – and more – at Ontario Hockey League games as most kids spent watching TV, doing homework, and going to parties. When I look back now, it feels like I grew up watching him play.

In 1993, Todd was drafted by the New York Islanders in the first round of the NHL draft. Between 1993 and 1995, I was able to finish college while he finished the last two of his four years of junior hockey. In September of 1995, at the ripe old age of twenty, we moved to Long Island, where he began his NHL career. That was just the first of many moves. We were married in 1996. Todd has played on several teams since then, and we've enjoyed every aspect of the hockey life. He was selected to play in two NHL all-star games and chosen to play for Team Canada in the 2004 Olympics in Torino, Italy. I have been lucky enough to watch him for all of these years and have been blessed enough to be able to stay home to raise our budding hockey stars.

I am the proud Hockey Mom of two players. When our daughter, Jaden, was in the fifth grade, she came home from school one day and announced that she was going to play hockey. I looked at her, surprised, and suggested that we perhaps learn how to skate before we decide such a thing. The following Saturday, we dressed her up in her brother's hockey gear and away she went. Barely able to stand on skates, let alone shoot, she impressed the coach enough that he told my husband, "She has something . . ." That something was a bruised tailbone from all the falling she did her first day on the ice! But from then on, I drove her to the rink every week for skating lessons, and she suited up in her own gear to play hockey with her new team. She has never looked back and now has dreams of playing college hockey. Jaden is our beautiful and burly right winger. She is feisty and fast, and all five-foot-eleven of her is great at screening any goalie on a power play.

And then there is our son, Tag. He is a miniature version of his father but with my stellar looks. His hockey career began at the age of two when he started sleeping with his first stick. He has always had a passion for the game, and when he was old enough to go to AAA status, he did. Wanting to be like his father, he has dreams of playing in the NHL.

Let me tell you, there is a big difference between watching my husband play professionally (and there is not much I enjoy more than that) and watching my kids on the ice. When my children play, I feel a different type of anxiety, and at times I even turn into one or another of the nuttier Hockey Moms you'll read about in the coming pages. All in all though, being a Hockey Mom is one of the most rewarding things I've done. It might sound lame to some, but I like nothing better than watching my children follow their passions and play the game.

I wrote *Hockey Moms: Realities from the Rink* first and foremost because I wanted to recognize all the work that we Hockey Moms do for our budding hockey stars. It takes a ton of effort and dedication to the game to spend as much time as we do – day after day, night after night, weekend after weekend – cheering on or cheering up our kids. Hockey is a true passion for some kids, especially the ones who dream of playing in college, at the Olympics, or in the NHL. Others play the game just for exercise and fun. Either way, we're there to encourage them – and sometimes yell at them. We are there to drive them, feed them, buy them equipment, and get their skates sharpened. We are there to give them positive support but also, sometimes, tough love, because, believe it or not, our kids don't always have great games. At times we are their coach, their shoulder to cry on, and even their doctor, diagnosing and tending to injuries. We are their cheerleaders and their biggest fans. Whatever our role, we are, always and truly, Hockey Moms.

I also wanted to recognize the sacrifices we make so our kids can play the game. What happened to our Saturday morning coffee, watching the news in our PJs, with bed heads and zero makeup? *Ohhhhh, it's hockey.* What about Sunday evenings at home with the family gathered around the dinner table for a feast? *Hockey.* Plus, if you have a kid in hockey, all the expenses start to add up – never mind if you have a second or third child in the mix. I mean, sometimes a girl just wants a new pair of jeans but has to forgo them because of the monthly ice bill. I have known moms and dads who take second jobs and work constant overtime to support their child's passion. The cost of getting new skates, replacing shoulder pads, and buying new helmets to match a new team's colours usually means that parents have to sacrifice something, and most kids don't realize this. We give up things we'd really like to have or to do, and we also do things we don't especially want to. From the countless loads of smelly laundry, to the added trips to the rink to get the skates sharpened, to meals made and eaten on the go, a lot of what we moms do just flies under their radars.

Sometimes Hockey Moms' contributions are over-looked or overshadowed by what Hockey Dads do. Well moms, I'm here to make damn sure this stops happening. We need to celebrate what we bring to the hockey table. We may not tape our player's stick, or be able to tie our kid's skates tight enough, or know enough about "offside" to understand why the whistle keeps blowing, but none of that matters. What *does* matter is that we paid the ice bill so that Billy could play, missed our favourite reality TV show on Susie's practice night, and loved them before practice just as much as after – we even loved them through the nasty hockey-glove stink.

Our Hockey Mom dedication goes beyond words. Sometimes we are driven crazy by our love of the game. Our competitive spirits ignite, we apply our game faces, and we become true fans, night in and night out. Many of us may not know as much as Dad does about the game or be able to offer the same kind of advice he does – and, let's face it, the kids might not take us seriously if we did try to have a hockey chat with them – but none of this should faze us, ladies. Let's proclaim it! We are real, modern-day Hockey Mom heroines.

Momma Bear

Of all the Hockey Mom names in this book, some of which you will have heard before, this is the one I think I'll become rich and famous for coining. I had the pleasure of getting to know a Momma Bear early on in my son's career, when he was the ripe old age of eight. Sitting in a freezing cold rink, not knowing a single soul, watching a squirt-aged hockey game, I had my first Momma Bear sighting, and we soon became friends.

A Momma Bear is like the lady next door, the kind you'd never expect to have a fierce side. She is a cute, fun-loving, social gal. At the rink before games, she just hangs out, chatting and giggling with the other moms. She doesn't have any special quirks. No wild clothing. No purple highlights in her hair. She is just a nice woman enjoying the game. That is until her player has the puck and someone dares to skate toward him. He doesn't even have to be making a big play; if someone on the other team has the nerve to body check, trip, slash, or – God forbid – punch her cutie – oh Lordie! – Momma Bear is released. She'll let out a wild, intense grumble, often one that can be heard for miles around. This will quickly become a growl that's seems to be just noise until you suddenly make out the words "Get him, Freddy!" or, better yet, "Beat her ass, Sally!" The feral roar that the Momma Bear makes will sound like the vocals of an '80s hair band – think Mötley Crüe here, ladies. Sometimes the Momma Bear will stand up and scream, and she may even shake her wild mane while yelling.

After the play is over, her nerves calm right down. She settles back into her spot as a cutie-pie mom just watching a youth hockey game. She will go straight back to her usual business of offering gum or mints to her neighbouring moms and continue on as if nothing happened at all.

We can all probably admit that we're a tad guilty of acting like a Momma Bear from time to time. Moms have a protective instinct hardwired into us, and when something or someone tries to hurt our prince or princess we tend to lose our minds slightly.

You know who you are, Momma Bears, and I say rock on!

The
Drama
Queen

The Drama Queen

I now present to you the Drama Queen.

You won't find her on every team, but if a team does have one of these ladies, everybody knows her. She makes her presence felt in many ways, and once she's into the dynamic of the scene, she's all in – with the good, the bad, and the ugly sides of her – whether at a tournament, a regular-season game, or even at a practice.

You may not recognize the Drama Queen Mom when you initially encounter her. On first sighting, she seems to be a quiet soul, standing off by herself, pretending to work on her cellphone. But what she's really doing is covertly observing the other moms to see who will be the perfect companion once she starts shit-disturbing. She'll prey on the more subdued ladies among us so that she can take the leading role, because what she really wants is a pal who can be her Side-Show Sally, but who won't steal her Oscar.

She ditches her not-saying-boo act quickly, and in no time she becomes a Chatty Cathy. At game time, she sits among the other moms, acting all soft-spoken and peaceful. That lasts until a player makes a move or a referee calls a play she doesn't quite agree with. Then she mumbles something under her breath that nobody can really hear. Eventually, she just can't help herself, or so she says later, and she starts speaking out loudly enough that her fellow moms, and everyone else around her, now find her very audible. In fact, she's in complete control of her entire routine, which might then involve nudging the unsuspecting mom she's picked to be her sidekick, coercing that poor lady's silent agreement with whatever outlandish statement she's making. Drama Queen may use hand actions as well, and, when she does, look out! You don't want to become a victim of her flailing arms and wind up with a black eye. She will also start standing up a lot – bolting up and then sitting back down – commanding attention that she suddenly seems to be working very hard to get.

Drama Queen is often caught doing provocative things, such as telling everyone that her child is a much superior player to anyone else on the team. She will say this over and over and over – getting the attention of most other parents because what she's saying is so outrageous. Let's face it, the typical Drama Queen doesn't know shit about hockey but thinks she's smarter than most coaches.

Sometimes, she waits to start the drama until she is at an away tournament, in the lobby of the hotel, when she's had a drink or five. Then she preaches to the many other drunken ears about her child's God-given talents. You've never seen a kid who is better at toe dragging or stick handling, and her player surely will be named MVP this weekend, yet again. But ladies, watch closely here because she's still just working up steam. The classic Drama Queen act usually comes the following day. By the time of the Sunday finals this mom is tired. But after her team's overtime loss, all hell breaks loose. She makes it known that, in her eyes, had her player, otherwise known as Baby Booboo, played the entire sixty minutes of the game, the team would have won gold. *Obviously.*

Let's keep in mind another couple of things about the Drama Queen. She seems unpredictable at first, but her skits become predictable after you've seen them a few times. Or mostly predictable. You never know if, in response to a penalty call on her player, she's going to scream or laugh or cry. The only thing you can be sure about is that, like it or hate it, you'll never have a dull moment when she's at her finest.

While some people may get slightly, or grossly, annoyed by this mom, most of us get a kick out of the

Drama Queen, for two reasons. One, she makes us laugh. Two, she takes attention away from our own crazed yelling at the ref. In other words, she acts so ridiculously that she makes the rest of us look extremely normal in comparison.

Recorder Mom

"Do you have your hockey bag?" Mom shouts from the kitchen. "Did you grab your jerseys?"

Yes, Mom.

"Sticks?"

Got 'em.

"Okay, hurry, meet me in the minivan. I just need to grab my video camera and I will be right out!"

And out comes Recorder Mom with her arms full of camera equipment, tripod and all. Whether she's got a camera stand, a suction cup camera for shots she'll take from behind the nets, or a shoulder sling to help her hold her recorder for three straight periods (seriously, lady, these days, any tablet or smartphone will do the trick), Recorder Mom is ready for action. She parks herself at the best vantage point and starts the camera rolling.

Why do these particular moms record practices and games? Not just the odd one, but *every single one*? Okay, do it once in a while if your kid is a goalie who needs extra work on positioning, and by all means do it at a gold-medal game in a tournament. You can even record for your husband on occasion, if he's away. But why do it all the time? Die-hard Recorder Moms tape practices, scrimmages, and even warm-ups, for God's sake. Their video obsession stumps me.

What I can't quite figure out is what she does with the videos. Does she watch them and take notes? Because if she does I have news for her: *Recorder Mom, Jonny has a coach. It's not you, and he really doesn't listen to your deafening hockey talk anyway.* Or does Recorder Mom use her videos as evidence to justify grounding her child? Like, if Jonny didn't work hard enough or skate fast enough, Recorder Mom will seize his cellphone for a week. It could be that Recorder Mom uses the video to comb through her player's shifts, ice time, and specialty team work, looking for details to bring up with the coach. But that can't really be it, because most moms know that going to the coach with complaints about things like that will get Jonny cut from the team next season. One last possibility is that Recorder Mom tapes everything so that she can watch it later, over a glass of wine on the couch, in her PJs, because she missed the live action while she was recording it at the game. That must be it.

The excessive documenting seems odd and, yes, a tad ridiculous to me. Sure, we all video our kids' plays now and again, but there have to be Hockey Mom video standards. *Please.* It's fun to be able to re-watch the exciting hockey moments – and not-so-great moments – caught on video. But let's not get carried away.

To all the Recorder Moms, I mean no offence here. I'd hate to take a ten-minute for unsportsmanlike conduct! If anything, I feel that we all suffer at times from a bit of Recorder Mom regret. In an exciting moment of play, I often say to myself, *Damn you. Why didn't you bring your camera?* On the flip side of that, of course, are the times when I do haul out my smartphone and decide to capture a moment. It always goes bad. Every time – and it never fails – that my son is about to do a shoot-out, I whip out my camera to record the goal, and every time he misses. When I consciously decide *not* to video the dangle, my super studly son scores! Go figure.

The Yodeller

I love this lady, and for a good reason: I may suffer – okay,
I *do* suffer – from this Hockey Mom syndrome, like I do
many others.

Picture this: It's an intense game. The score is close.
The play is fast and gritty. There are lots of moms sitting in
the stands, and one is a Yodeller. For the moment, she's just
watching the game. Only when her baby does a sweet toe
drag, sets up an awesome play, or passes in a dangerous
direction does the humming begin. It starts calmly enough,
with a soft noise at the back of her throat. But as soon as
the play intensifies, the Yodeller's voice follows suit. The
yodel becomes higher and stronger, and, as the game goes
on, the Yodeller uses different pitches and tones. Exactly
what they sound like depends on the particular mom and

the quality of the game. Her yodel can range from fairly faint to deafeningly loud. It is not uncommon for this mom to wrap herself in a blanket, which she'll hold to her mouth to muffle her sounds. Sometimes the yodel is simply meant as a cheer, sometimes it's a complaint, and at other times it comes out at a low pitch, with a variation in tone I can only guess is meant to settle her nerves after a gruelling two minutes of play.

It is important to note that sometimes the Yodeller Mom uses her voice just to release some stress without sounding like a Hockey Mom who has a potty mouth. In most cases these ladies don't even realize they are doing it. Some of them manage to yodel in a whisper so quiet it can hardly be heard.

I should also mention here another Hockey Mom type – the Woo Mom, who, like the Yodeller, will use different sounds for different plays. For example, if a goal is scored, it's a full on *wooooo hoooooooo*. If a goal is saved, it's a *whoooooooooosh*. The extremely excited, on-her-feet, extended *woooooooooooooooooooo* is reserved for overtime goals, comeback goals, and championship wins. She has a low, droning *woo* for tense situations, a medium-level *woo* for an average pass or play, and a high-pitched, full-volume WOO for a great play. The *woos* also differ depending on whether she's cheering for her player or someone else's child. Her player always gets the loudest *woo*. This woman has been known to *woo* so hard she *woos* herself right off the bench she's sitting on. Believe it or not, there is also the Accidental Woo Mom, who *woos* at all the wrong times because she's confused and knows next to nothing about the game. But good for her for showing up and cheering. Keep coming and keep *woooohooooing*!

Big Mouth Betty

It only takes one listen, and after that you will instantly recognize Big Mouth Betty, anytime, anywhere. Her distinctive shriek can be heard the moment you enter the rink's lobby. She is the mom who acts like she's played a thousand games in the NHL, even though she has never actually worn a pair of skates. Or, if she has played the game, she likely gained all of her hockey knowledge during her old college days. She just doesn't know that the game has changed dramatically since the 1990s. Perhaps she's learned everything she knows in the lobbies of the great many arenas she has seen. She may even have taught herself by watching NHL network game highlights over breakfast. Whatever odd place is the source of her hockey wisdom, she's certainly not shy in telling you all about it.

She takes over most conversations, and she is always right when it comes to the game of hockey. There's no point even trying to talk hockey with Big Mouth Betty because you will never be right – unless, that is, she agrees with you.

This Hockey Mom always stands with the same circle: either with the ladies who are used to her or with her own children, who have no choice but to hang out with her at the rink. Sometimes you will see her with that one nice mom who just accepts everybody, but most of the team parents try to avoid her. Even her own husband tries to get out of going to the games with her. Or he chooses to stand by the glass, on the opposite side of the rink, so he can't hear her yakking.

One difference between Big Mouth Betty and other Hockey Moms is that most moms don't want to be "that parent" constantly in the coach's face expressing one or several opinions on every matter. But because Betty is such a hockey guru, the other parents quite often suggest to her that she take her beef about the team's business to the coach. She can also be "loud" on email, sending out "reply alls" with her comments on the previous night's game. These are a little easier to ignore.

Like the Drama Queen, this mom can be heard throughout the game. But unlike the Drama Queen, who's busy waving her arms in the air, Big Mouth Betty keeps active by constantly colour commentating the play. At times she feels she really needs to help coach, after all. And this is no act. She truly can't help herself. So she steps right into Coach Mom's role and calls out the next line rotation or screams at her kid to get his head out of his ass so that he can see the play. Worse, she's unafraid to insult any player on the ice: forward, defence, or goalie. She yells at refs, she shouts at linesmen, and she has been known to holler at other moms too. She gets especially fired up at dirty plays, so much so that other moms sometimes have to relocate to different seats in the middle of a period.

Quick tip ladies: always be the last to the bleachers. Let Big Mouth Betty get in first and stake out her area, and then you can find a different place to sit. And one last word of advice: limit this women to *one* large coffee, as caffeine is the last thing she needs. God forbid she has a beer or a glass of red before a game.

THE ROAD TRIP:
PACKING AND RITUALS

THE ROAD TRIP: PACKING AND RITUALS

Is it just me or does it also seem to all of you moms that going away for a three-day tournament feels like going away for a week? As Hockey Moms, we have a tremendous amount of responsibility when it comes to travelling for away games and tournaments. Our kids take us for granted, of course, and assume that we will bring everything they could possibly want or need for the next few days. Unlike a dad, who would probably pack a pair of jeans, a toothbrush, and a case of beer, we moms are prepared for anything.

Let's start with the suitcase. If you're anything like me, three days before you leave you've got your player's outfit for each day cleaned and laid out, ready to be packed. Warm-up suit: *check*. Socks: *check*. PJs: *check*. Hockey bag and sticks: *check*. Plus, don't forget the homework. For some strange reason, even before I get the suitcases out, I feel that I must wash every piece of dirty laundry in the house. I also have to clean the entire house before I go, even though I know from experience that whoever is staying behind will launch a grenade in it the minute

I leave. I wash every single dish and stow it away. I buy
the groceries and make enough dinners for everyone left
at home to eat, and put them in the fridge, which is where
I find them upon my return – all still in the fridge – because
everyone who stayed home thought it would be fun to eat
out after they tossed the grenade.

Once we get going, whether we're travelling alone or
with friends, we try to bring some method to the madness
of road trips. One season, I spent a lot of time in a car with
another Hockey Mom, whom we dubbed Louise, as in the
movie *Thelma and Louise*. I was Thelma because I was
the driver and was always behind the wheel. Each trip, we'd
set up our boys in the back with the video game console in
full Play mode, Louise and I would tune into the '80s XM
satellite station, and away we'd go, singing at the top of our
lungs. The boys would chime in every now and then, either
trying to shut us up or singing along. By the fifth hour of
most trips that year, we would become a tad delirious and
start calling the boys names like Vinnie (because he's Italian)
and Joey Dirt (to go with the straggly, long blond hair).
We always had a ton of fun – on the way there.

But the fun lasted only as long as the team was
winning, and that particular season our boys, as good as
they were, were having a hard time getting the gold. So,
at one weekend tournament, Louise and I decided to take
matters into our own hands and start a pre-game ritual.

It was the middle of the winter in what seemed like the middle of the night, though in actuality it was six in the morning and we were on our way to the quarter-finals game. With the boys nestled in the back seat, we drove until we found a farmer's field. After making sure that there was no one around, we buttoned up our parkas and pulled up our boots, got the boys out of the car, and all four of us lay down in the snow and made angels. We laughed and laughed, and, go figure, we won that morning's game. So, before the semi-finals, we made our way back to the same farmer's field and "angeled" our brains out. And, we won – again! We were moving on to the finals. The morning of the game, we drove back to the farmer's field. We made so many snow angels, there couldn't have been more than a square inch of fresh snow left on the field.

This was our year of being the bridesmaid, however. After our third trip to the farmer's field, we lost. We never were the bride that season. We always got to the finals, but we just could not win. So we never made snow angels again, because it didn't work for the win.

The ride home that weekend was totally toned down. We packed in our Thelma and Louise personas and spent the drive debating with our boys about whether, for the next tournament, we should change up our names, rituals, or food choices – whatever would bring us the gold.

Princess Mom

Goddamn, girl!

Who cares if this mom does or doesn't know what icing is? She looks good. Always. Princess Mom lives up to her name if by nothing else then by the clothes on her back, her high heels, her big, fully styled hair, and her perfectly applied makeup. We have all seen her at games, at practice, at off-ice workouts – it doesn't matter where. What does matter, at least to her, is how she looks. This mom is, at all times, done up. She is *on*.

Princess Mom often opts to wear a glittery shirt, occasionally one that has the words *Hockey Mom* spangled across her boobs. She wears high-heeled boots to go with her skin-tight jeans, which usually have beading or rhinestones on the bum to coordinate with her sparkling shirt.

Princess Mom is often a combo mom, as she's rarely just a pretty face. She can also be a Big Mouth Betty, with her perfectly lined lips really flapping away if the game calls for it. Sometimes she's also a Momma Bear, but her hairspray keeps her immaculately coiffed lid intact during her occasional, vigorous head shakes.

Now, don't get me wrong; I do appreciate the effort she puts in to looking good, especially because I enjoy showing up at the rink with no makeup on and in my sweats – although after standing beside Princess Mom I tend to feel that maybe I should have made an effort and at least have put on some lipstick. On occasion, I've even gone home after a game spent next to her and had a long chat with myself about getting my act together and stopping with the laziness. I end up resolving to wear my nice clothes to the rink for a change instead of ones that are meant for lounging in the privacy of my own home or for doing yoga.

Then I start to wonder how long she takes to get herself ready and whether this process ever interferes with her player's sleep when they are away at a tournament. After all, ladies, we don't stay at the Ritz. The hotel rooms tend to be small, and if she's getting up at five in the morning to blast the blow dryer over her hair for thirty minutes, it could hinder her player's shut-eye. Combine the roar of the dryer with the buzz of the airbrush machine she uses to apply her foundation, the clacking of makeup brushes, and the hissing of an aerosol can spewing out maximum-hold hairspray, and it would suggest to me that her angel isn't exactly sleeping as snug as a bug.

I admit that not all Princess Moms are so extreme. Some moms just like to look nice, glittery shirt or not. Some Princess Moms do not feel the need to go all out in the hair and makeup department, but even half-painted they always look great. True, we can't quite call this mom a full-blown Princess Mom, but she can be called a Duchess Mom. Which is not to be confused with a Douche Mom – that's a mom for a whole different book. Regardless of her handle, you'll never see this mom *au natural*. That would strip her of her title and possibly of her self-esteem.

All in all, I say keep on applying your lipstick and wearing your heels, Princess Moms – we admire you!

Ref Basher

What can I say about the Ref Basher that you don't already know? She's quite simple. She just can't stand any call these guys make. It doesn't matter if the ref is right or wrong. The second his hand goes up, she starts to holler. She will often refer to the refs as "Stripes" and will happily yell rehearsed insults, such as, "Hey, Stripes, get off your knees. You're blowing a good game!" or "When you get home make sure you check your answering machine because you've been missing calls all day!" And, my personal favourite, "Hey, Ref, give your head a shake, your eyes are stuck!"

She is so against the ref, no matter who he is, that she's cursing him before she realizes he only raised his arm for an icing, not because her innocent player just happened to two-hand a kid across the back of his legs.

Ref Basher busts a breast screaming at Stripes over every call. The refs are damned if they do and damned if they don't. Whenever the ref does make a penalty call, good or bad, the veins in Ref Basher's neck start to jut out and she turns bright red.

Ref Basher Mom doesn't like to be alone in her opinions though, and she knows how to drag anyone near her into her madness. She will say, "Oh my God, did you see that?" Or, "Holy shit, I can't believe he called that!" Which in turn gets you fired up, and pretty soon you're angry at the ref too!

What can you do to stay calm? Not much. You can't argue with her because she's always right and the ref is always wrong. It's better just to avoid the scene. When you see the Ref Basher's veins starting to pop, it's a great time to get up and use the ladies' room, whether you need to or not.

Hard to
Please
Mom

Hard to Please Mom

Here is the mom who loves to shop – not at the mall, but at the rink. Hard to Please Mom isn't looking to buy anything. She's just constantly shopping *her player*.

At the start of each season, this mom is so happy. Nothing could be better for her than a new team and fresh faces. *This* is the season of all promise and no disappointments. But by Christmas her shopping starts, and it has nothing to do with what Santa will deliver. It's December and Hard to Please Mom has had enough. Again. She needs to find a new coach and a team that is better suited for her all-star. Never mind that her child gets injured on almost a weekly basis, taking a dramatic fall from which she gets up very slowly, if she gets up at all. At first you worry that the kid will never walk again, only for her to have a miraculous recovery and play the next shift, if she's called upon. By the third time she gets hit, you've stop worrying. Instead, you're wondering where the kid learned such a thing.

According to Hard to Please Mom, her child is usually played "unfair minutes," or she "gets short shifted" and is always "left off the power play" whenever a goal is needed. As soon as you hear this kind of talk from Hard to Please Mom, you know the schmoozing is about to start. At every subsequent game, you'll see her chatting it up with the opposing team's coach or parents, trying to finagle her player's way onto a new team – even if it means moving to a new city or state.

Certain Hard to Please Moms are spotted at every hockey-skills camp and holiday clinic, and at private skates in every corner of the map. She will expose her child to whatever she must in order to have her seen and heard. Hard to Please Mom will brag nonstop about the personal trainer she hired for her player, or the power-skating coach young Kelly is seeing to prepare for the scholarship that she is guaranteed to receive. More often than not, this mom will turn out to have a dark secret: she has never played a sport in her life. She has never experienced true competition, but she wants to, and so she's doing it vicariously through her child.

Now don't get me wrong here; although the Hard to Please Mom is rarely satisfied, she does deserve a lot of credit for the effort and passion that she puts into her player. At least she cares, even if it is all a little too much.

Grandmom

God bless these women. There are so many of them who haul themselves out to games every week to cheer on their grandkids, and I salute them all.

After her morning workout at Curves, the Hockey Grandmom will sit on her rocker and count down the hours and minutes until it's time to leave for the rink. There, you can often spot her in the lobby before the game, making her rounds and saying hello to everyone. She is likely decked out in hockey paraphernalia and carrying a handmade blanket with her team's colours on full display. On week nights, you'll often see a large contingent of these older ladies at the game – a lot of them are retired and don't have to go to work the next day. If you're lucky, among them you will find a

Grandmom Ref Basher, Yodeller, and Super Clapper too.

At every game, when I gaze around the rink, I see Hockey Grandmoms in all shapes and sizes, decorated proudly: team pins on their hats, buttons of the grand-darlings on their scarves, and sometimes wearing a bedazzled sweatshirt with "hockey grandmom" spelled out in rhinestones. Most of them have wonderful stories about toting their boys or girls from rink to rink, back in the day. They talk about how the game used to be very different. There weren't any off-ice workouts an hour before the game. There were fewer whistles because the refs let a lot more slide, and, by the way, people didn't used to be so hypersensitive about every less-than-complimentary remark made in the stands. After all, a Grandmom once told me, this is hockey, not etiquette class.

That being said, these hockey Grandmoms are fiercely protective of their grandchildren. They have zero problem yelling at or even cursing the ref if one so much as attempts to make a bad call on their precious player. This unreserved behaviour, in the form of Grandmom Big Mouth Betty shouting at another teammate – almost always negatively – usually results in their daughters relocating to another seat, and their daughters' husbands too, for that matter.

It doesn't matter whether these amazing Grandmoms know anything about how hockey is played these days;

they still show up game after game and always smile when they see their players. These are proud ladies who love their grandkids, win, lose, or tie.

Super Clapper Mom

Have you ever sat in the stands of an old barn arena and heard every whistle, cheer, and clap echo around the place? Even a brand new, state-of-the-art facility with an aluminum ceiling can make the sound of a hard clap reverberate.

The Super Clapper Mom is one of those moms who knows nothing, or next to nothing, about hockey, so to show her support she just claps. Good play or bad, she claps. Icing or offside, she claps. Penalty or bad pass – again – she claps. When she thinks she sees her player's team score, she speeds up the pace of her applause. But she's quick to cut the super clap short when she looks around and notices that it's actually the opposing team that put the puck in the net and scored. To recover, she picks back up with a few one-time claps just so it appears she meant to clap either way.

If you close your eyes and listen to the Super Clapper, you will be able to gauge the game's pace of play. The tempo of her claps is timed to the action on the ice and to the misery of losing a poorly played game. But, fast or slow, she is always putting her hands together and yanking them apart, slapping silly. This is why, after the game, you will often see Super Clapper Mom in the rink lobby drenching her red palms in moisturizer.

There are, however, some Super Clapper Moms who *do* know a thing or two about hockey. These moms are passionate about the game and choose to express themselves through the sound of applause rather than spouting their mouths off like the Ref Basher or Big Mouth Betty. Come to think of it, with all of these Hockey Moms in the stands, we could form a band. The Super Clapper Mom would be the percussion section, Momma Bear and Big Mouth Betty the lead singers, and the Ref Basher could do back up vocals. With the Leaner Mom swaying like a dancer and Foreign Express Mom acting like a groupie in furs, we'd be huge.

THE DREADED CAR RIDE
AFTER A LOSS

THE DREADED CAR RIDE AFTER A LOSS

We've all had them: the dreaded car ride home after a bad game. Let's relive those times for a moment. It will be therapeutic.

So, your player had a bad game. You and your hubby watched the whole thing, unfortunately, and now in the lobby afterwards, close-mouthed, the two of you are waiting for your player to emerge from the dressing room with his head down. If the kid played really badly, your husband will have foregone the lobby wait altogether and headed straight to the car.

The walk of shame from the rink to the car is done in silence. Your player's head is still down, mainly because he's deciding whether to try to walk home or to bite the bullet and get into the minivan. Actually, your husband has already entertained the thought of making the lad walk home because, in his recollection, that's what his dad would have suggested to him back in the day. After everyone has finally piled in, and the smelly hockey bag has been stashed in the trunk, you do your best to sound sweet as you ask if everyone has their seatbelts on. You needn't have tried, as you are met only with silence or a sullen groan, meaning yes, from the back seat. The drive begins, and all your player can really hope for is that his younger sibling, who was at the game that night, behaved worse in the stands than your player played his game.

The tension builds with every minute and every turn of the road, but eventually your husband explodes. He can't help himself. He has to yell because he wants more from his son, wants him to give his all at every game. This is typically your player's breaking point. All he can think is, Why didn't I walk home? He may or may not be in tears now; if he is, your inner Momma Bear starts to wake up. All *you* can think of doing is defending your poor baby. By this time, everyone in the car is shouting, the defroster is on to keep the windows from fogging up, and, if it's really bad, the whole car is shaking.

In this situation, you're lucky if you live close to the arena. Your husband can get home quickly and have a beer to help him settle down, and the poor kid can sneak off to bed. If your player's lucky, the drive takes about fifteen minutes. That's just long enough for your husband to get tired from all his screaming and for you to have started arguing with him in defence of your baby. This spousal spat releases your child from his pickle and he is off scot-free.

If you're unlucky, the drive home takes two hours. The "advice" your husband is bawling gets repeated at least ten times before the ride is over, and almost as loudly the tenth time as the first. In the extreme, he will recount the whole game as he saw it and explain what your child should have done on every shift. This sometimes ends up with your young guy muttering under his breath that he should have gone home with another family.

Despite it all, everyone climbs back into the van the next night to do it over again. That's how much you love each other, and hockey.

Payoff Mom

"Okay, Sally, if you score a hat trick I will buy you a puppy."

"Here's the deal, Mikey: You get twenty dollars for every goal you score."

I'm not making it up. These kinds of promises are real. This wheeling and dealing actually happens – all the time. And if you hear this kind of offer coming out of your own mouth, or someone else's, you either are, or you are in close contact with, a Payoff Mom: the mom who wants the win more than her child does, for Facebook bragging rights or the next day's water cooler discussion about what a superstar her child is.

Imagine sitting in the bleachers at an out-of-town tournament. It's the final game, and your child has already played five. All the Hockey Moms and Hockey Dads – not to mention the players – are exhausted, but emotions are high because it's possible you will go home champions. Moms everywhere are buzzing with excitement and nerves. Then, you overhear the mom next to you saying that she has told her player that if he wins the tournament he won't have to go to school the next day. Another mom chimes in: "Oh, I told my kid that if they win, I'll take him to any restaurant he wants to eat at for a week."

One serial Payoff Mom told me that if her superstar sniper scored during that game, he would get a new stick. A $250-dollar, fiberglass stick, just for a goal, and just after he was given a new one following the last tournament, when his mom made the same deal with him. It's crazy that players should want to score for anything other than the love of the game. Although, if someone were to offer me a payoff for sitting in the stands and jeering, I would happily become a Big Mouth Betty for a new pair of jeans!

Okay, if I'm going to be honest, I may be guilty of having been a Payoff Mom on a few occasions. I remember making a deal with my sweet pea that if she scored a hat trick I would buy her a sweater that was on her wish list. She came awfully close and scored two goals that game. Even though she didn't hold up her end of the deal, I caved and bought her the sweater anyway. And my son and I do have a standing arrangement of a sort. I promised him that, whenever he wins gold, he can eat at McDonald's (he is not offered this food on a regular basis). So every time we win a tournament, you'll find the two of us under Mickey Dee's golden arches, binge eating Big Macs and super-size servings of fries.

Team Manager Mom

First things first: let's not confuse this woman with Coach Mom – the mom you'll always find behind the bench.

If anyone is in any doubt about who the Team Manager Mom is, you can easily point her out. She is the woman wearing a team jacket, probably with the word *manager* embroidered just above her left boob. She is the mom carrying a file folder stuffed with all of the team's paperwork and game sheets. She is the mom who does her best to make things easy for the rest of us Hockey Moms and Dads.

Team Manager Mom's duties likely include charting plus–minuses and shots on net; she pays the refs and coordinates team meals, books events, and supplies the Gatorade. She sends weekly email updates to the parents, answers all of our dumb questions, and collects our hard-earned money to pay the ice bills. She is efficient, super organized, and very good at her tasks. She takes her job seriously and enjoys it, which is why it is almost impossible for her to give it up or let herself be released from duty if her child quits or gets cut from the team.

That said, you should note that Team Manager Moms vary in the degree of effort they put into their jobs. Some are excellent at getting other parents to volunteer for some of the work, and some are total control freaks who insist on doing every job themselves. One way or the other, these women are multitaskers, and they work tirelessly. They deserve a huge Christmas present or an end-of-season gift card – without their having to organize it!

There is another *crucial* function that the Team Manager Mom fulfills. She's the mom who books hotel rooms for all of the away tournaments, a lot of times at crappy hotels in order to keep down the costs of being away so much. You won't find a hotel bar or a piano man at most of these places, but we parents still need a place we can get together to unwind after the game. The blessed Team Manager Mom is always sure to ask the hotel manager for a room where we won't be hassled for drinking our own booze. A good Team Manager Mom will make sure this sacred place is far away from the one hundred kids playing mini sticks on the second floor and the seventy-five other kids playing tag on the elevators. She will do whatever it takes to get us this room, as she's often first in line to get wasted. Team Manager Mom is very businesslike, but when her tasks for the day are completed, she's the most in need of some rest and relaxation, and often winds up being the drunkest parent in the hotel drinking room. But don't judge her. This is purely a stress-relieving alcohol binge. The Team Manager Mom has a taxing volunteer position. The following day, she'll be back to business as usual, crushing headache or not.

Practice Mom

Have you ever gone to the rink with your son or daughter
for practice and just chit-chatted with some of the other
moms, paying little attention to what's happening on the
ice? I know I have. But, as you have likely noticed, there
are some moms who sit through every practice. Some
watch every drill and water break, and listen for the coach's
whistle. Others enjoy taking in a bit of the action as they
leaf through the pages of *People* magazine.

The question is, why?

Let's imagine the most likely scenario. Perhaps Practice
Mom is taking mental notes so that when her player gets
into the car she can pull out her dry-erase board and go
through everything he did wrong. Now that's something
I would pay Recorder Mom to catch on film. Imagine

watching a Practice Mom trying to rerun the whole workout in her Volvo, steaming up the windows, all while her player is wolfing down chocolate milk and a protein bar and wishing he was home already. Do you think this mom could be discussing with her kid how he did certain drills, or his level of effort? And if she is, does she suppose her player is actually listening to what she has to say after skating his guts out for ninety minutes? My bet is he's not. I would also put twenty dollars on the line to wager that if Practice Mom tried to bring up a particular drill with her player, he would more than likely just stick in his earbuds and pretend that the lecture wasn't actually happening.

My advice to all of the Practice Moms out there – actually, to *all* Hockey Moms out there – is not to bother with the teaching and the lecturing. Leave coaching solely to the coach! It's always wiser to just get in the car and ask how practice was, as if you had watched the whole thing without actually taking in the particulars. That way, you're totally off the hook and don't have to be a Negative Nancy about every little thing Jimmy did wrong. You attended practice like a good mom, but you too were busy gossiping with the other moms to be able to give your boy a hard time. And when he asks, "Mom, did you see my sick shoot-out goal?" you enthusiastically nod your head and say, "Yes, babe. You are amazing. That was awesome!"

Foreign Express Mom

Here we have a mom who has moved her life, job, family – *everything* – for her little all-star's hockey career. The all-star who is eleven years old. He likely has serious potential to be drafted into the NHL, so it's totally worth it. To some. Really. It happens sometimes. Other times, it doesn't, which is the more likely scenario.

Though socially she may be one of the more reserved among us, Foreign Express Mom is definitely not shy in the stands. She will do a lot of shouting – in Russian, Swedish, Finnish, or *Swinglish*, which is all or any of the above languages – occasionally other ones – tied in with a few English words here and there. With her strong accent and powerful Slavic or Scandinavian vocal tones, Foreign Express Mom's screams sound weirdly beautiful.

It's not that she doesn't speak perfectly good English, and fluently, no less. It's just that she often ignores the common folk until she's ready to say something, then perfect English rolls off her tongue. Foreign Express Mom may even mix up her languages on purpose so the rest of us don't hear the obscenities she uses to berate the players and the refs on the ice. Out of the stands, this otherwise quiet woman revs herself up to full throttle when young Vladimir gets into the car after a bad game. The windows almost shatter as they rattle from the sound of Foreign Express Mom's screeches as she lets little Vladi know that she will not tolerate his lack of effort, or poor play, or both.

Most North American women stay warm at the rinks by wearing long, hooded puffer coats. The beautiful, European, Foreign Express Mom most often turns up in a mink or sable coat. She is not the slightest bit afraid of folks who frown upon the real fur deal. And no one gives her a hard time anyway, because this mom can be one intimidating *chica*. We know better than to mess with a Foreign Express Mom. She has invested a lot of money and made huge changes in her life for the sake of her child's future in hockey, so you know she means business. Hockey Moms everywhere, Be kind at all costs to these women. Accept their *Swinglish*, pet their fur coats, and give them a pat on the back for being so dedicated.

The
Leaner

The Leaner

The woman I am referring to here is the mom who leans from side to side or front to back, depending on which way her player is carrying the puck. We've all seen her. However, if you yourself are a leaner, you may not be able to pick another one like you out of the crowd because you're too busy swaying in your seat.

The Leaner's signature move is to tilt to one side as she tracks her player's rush down the ice. If her kid's not on the ice and not involved in the play, she won't move too much. Rarely does she sway when her player's line isn't on, but a close score may get the Leaner rocking, no matter who's playing. Overtime takes the Leaner to a whole new level of motion. If she was sitting down during the game, she'll more than likely be standing for overtime. When she's on her feet, she's strictly a side-to-side gal, because she knows that to go forward and backward would only land her head first in the bleachers.

Ladies, I have a confession to make: I am a Leaner. There, I said it. I am aware that I'm a habitual Leaner. I tilt from side to side, back to front, and I sometimes go around in a full circle. Not only am I a Leaner but, when the game is close, I sometimes go as far as to cover my face with my blanket while leaning and I may even let out an indelicate yodel from time to time. It's quite the combo.

Something you should be especially aware of: if you happen to be sitting next to a Leaner, you'll quickly find out that she's often a Grabber or a Slapper too. If the game is really intense, or if she is very involved in the play, the Leaner may alternately swat and put a vise grip on the people seated next to her. And won't even know she's doing so until the whistle blows and she finds someone's jacket sleeve bunched up in her fist. She'll apologize, only to do the same thing again – time after time, game after game.

You need to know who the Grabbers, the Slappers, and the Leaners are because, if you're sitting next to one of them, you run the risk of leaving the game bruised and battered, and you should know what to expect in advance. If you're smacked, remember that it's not a personal attack. The Leaner is just so wrapped up in the game that she doesn't realize she's hit you. Do not be tempted to smack her back. I wish you luck if you're unfortunate enough to have a Learner, or a Slapper, or even a Grabber on both sides. And if you have a habit of surrounding yourself with these passionate moms, you may want to invest in some elbow and shoulder pads to avoid injury.

POSITIVITY

POSITIVITY

Although there are a ton of tournament weekends I'd like to forget, this one was memorable. We named it the Weekend of Positivity.

It was, once again, an away tournament, and my player and I travelled with another Hockey Mom and her son. On our four-hour drive the night before the first game, my fellow mom and I decided that this was going to be the weekend of the win. In order to ensure victory, we told the boys, we were all going to be positive. Positive about anything and everything in our paths. They looked at us like we'd just bounced our heads off a concrete wall, but we didn't let that get us down.

Our initial challenge came the next morning, before the first game, when we were served the hotel's continental breakfast. It consisted of artificial eggs on cold bagels. After we gave up trying to eat it, we decided that everything was still okay. Breakfast had been terrible, but the game was going to be great, because when you think positive thoughts, great things happen. Although our boys were starving and thirsty, it just didn't matter. We were going to win. And guess what? We did! So after game one, it was easy to convince the boys to believe in our theory of positivity. We hopped into the car and sang church hymns and praised everything we could think of. Lunch was absolutely delicious, and soon we were back, ready for game two. We told the boys that, no matter what happened next, they were amazing. Life was too short not to have fun, we said, and we advised them just to have a great game.

What do you know, but that afternoon, at game two, we had another win. Boy, were we on to something. That was it for day one of the tournament. We ate a delicious dinner, and the boys went to bed early. The next day was going to be even better than the first day had been.

At five in the morning we got our wake-up call. It was bitterly cold outside – and I mean absolutely frigid – but everything was perfect in our little world. The auto start on the truck wouldn't work from the hotel entrance, which was an eight-mile jaunt from where we had parked. God, where was the parking valet when we needed him? When we reached the truck, nose hairs frozen together and icicles hanging off our eyebrows, we drove straight to the nearest Starbucks for a quick bite, only to discover that it didn't open until six. Our next option was the McDonald's drive-through, but the lineup there was ten cars long, which to a little boy looks like a wait of more than an hour.

Besides, we had to be at the rink in five minutes. Off we went to 7-Eleven, an all-time low, but it didn't matter. We had embarked on day two of positive mania. We found day-old doughnuts for the boys and tarlike coffee for us adults, and off we went.

Game three was another success, despite the fact that my travelling partner's son, who was also our team's star defenceman, had started to feel quite ill and wasn't going anywhere except straight to the john, where he stayed. After a super-quick drive back to the hotel, we raced over to the local pharmacy and bought some Pepto-Bismol, which we made our ailing player drink – fast. We were on a roll, and no stupid stomach problem was going to ruin this weekend. Our guy had a nap and a pep talk and a pre-game poop, and we were off to game four. Okay, so we did decide to bypass the 7-Eleven and go straight to the rink this time. The whole way to the arena, we annoyed the boys with our positive vibrations and cheery chants. We were being just plain silly, but, oh my God, did we laugh.

The most amazing thing was that this being upbeat stuff really worked. We won that game too.

The following morning, bright and early, we set off for the quarter-finals. Sure, our team had a certain, not-so-stellar track record. Sure, we had checked out of the hotel and had our bags packed and stowed in the back in case we lost, but that wasn't spoken of to the children, because we were all about the positive. Our job was to keep the boys thinking that they were basically going to win the Stanley Cup that weekend.

But that was it. At game five, things went south. Even though we yelled out every positive chant and cheer we could think of, it didn't seem to matter. We lost. We were out of the tournament. We were going home losers, once again.

There really is no good way to sugarcoat a loss. We were mad, sad, disappointed, and ashamed. We made a ton of excuses for the loss and vowed that we would never try the positive baloney again, then settled in for a long, quiet drive home. Our players, on the other hand, managed to work out their frustrations by playing games on their X box the whole way. So, in the end, we were all happy.

The Freeloader

Oh, she's a beauty!

This mom is just as she's labelled, a freeloader. She is typically an outgoing, fun-loving gal who basically never drives anywhere, never pays for anything, and never offers to help anyone, anytime, in any way. The Freeloader is always polite when she asks for rides for her player to and from practice, to and from most games, and to and from all tournaments. Not only does she cop rides for her kid, but she jumps in as well. This way she never has to pay at the pump! During pit stops on the long journey, or at a team dinner, she will quietly suggest to the server that one bill is fine. Out the window goes the player number system. Then, when one bill comes, she discovers that – *oops!* – she accidentally left her wallet in the car or, better yet, at the hotel. This revelation more often than not is followed by her saying, "I'm so embarrassed. I'll pick up the check next time," or "I'll pay you as soon as I get my wallet." And she really means it. Her travel companions usually respond by saying, "No worries. It's all good." The Freeloader's charm has won again. She escapes without paying for yet another meal, and moves on to the next.

Here's a warning to you all: if you lend the Freeloader Mom money, she will never actually repay you, even though her repeated promises to do so convince you otherwise. She will also never offer to drive to a tournament or a game. Why would she? That is just not her style. What could be better than a free ride, listening to music, playing on her smartphone, and never even having to navigate?

Mental note here, girls: when I talk about the Freeloader Mom, I'm *not* referring to that heroic mom who sometimes has to lean on you for help due to her financial circumstances. This mom, otherwise known as Wicked Awesome Selfless Mom, deserves extra credit for doing whatever she can to make sure her player gets to every game, tournament, and off-ice session. She is *not* the Freeloader. She is a hard-working, double-jobbed, selfless mom, who works her ass off to pay for her angel's hockey. This awesome woman should be supported in whatever way she needs. If you can, go out of your way to offer her a lift now and then or treat her to a meal once in a while. No kid should miss out on hockey because his mom can't always afford the ice bills. Welcome Wicked Awesome Selfless Mom, ladies. Embrace her.

Coach Mom

Here we have the mom who, naturally, grew up playing hockey, and usually other sports too. Most Coach Moms have daughters who play on the team, and they have coached since the day their girls started playing. They coach only in girls' hockey leagues. At least I, for one, have never witnessed a female coach behind the bench on a boys' team, although it's probably happened somewhere. These women are tough and can tap into girls' emotions, as we all know men cannot! So when a female player comes into the dressing room crying, the Coach Mom presumes she is PMSing and offers her sympathy, whereas the Man Coach would just roll his eyes and walk away.

Most referees have a love-hate relationship with Coach Mom. Coach Mom generally knows hockey, but when she points out certain things to the ref, he tends not to listen as intently as he would to Man Coach – who usually doesn't like what he hears and ends up screaming. But, then again, some Coach Moms, with their high-pitched voices, will make the hair on the back of the ref's neck stand at every whistle. The refs appreciate that Coach Mom tends to have far more patience than the typical Man Coach. When the whistle blows and there is contention about the play, Coach Mom will wave the ref over, ask a few questions, and likely leave it at that, whether she agrees with the call or not. Compare that to a Man Coach. He will call the ref over, shout his questions in the ref's face, and, if he doesn't like the end result of their conversation, proceed to call the ref an M-F. Man Coach's hair-trigger approach and colourful language makes even the toughest Coach Moms seem like a dream.

Coach Mom wears many hats, and I'm not talking toques and fedoras here. She works all day, then she goes home and cooks dinner, makes lunches for the next day, and gets the family's laundry done, all before heading to practice. She also remembers to make sure the team's medical kit is stocked with tampons, Midol, and ponytail elastics.

Coach Mom is always decked out in team sweats, and at a certain point before the game she is more than likely to be found by the dressing room door, awaiting her moment to get in there and give her team a motivational speech, which she more than likely wrote while at her day job that afternoon. At her finest, Coach Mom will hand out props, such as Life Savers candies, with her speech. "Envision yourself as a life saver," she will say. "If your line mate needs your help, you will always be there to save her life." This well-intentioned motivational speech will slide right off the girls, because all they really want to do is eat the candy and possibly ask for another one before hitting the ice. Most of them will be well-mannered enough not to let Coach Mom hear them giggling to the point of tears inside their helmets. I seriously doubt any man would be brave enough to attempt such a speech.

All in all, I congratulate every Coach Mom for having the patience and perseverance to do her best to teach ours darling angels. Lord, help me.

Quiet Mom

Quiet Mom

Listen up here, *chicas*! Quiet Moms are a rare breed, and I have encountered only a few of these elusive ladies over many years. Could be because they hide out in their cars and read during the practices and games, or it could be that they don't come to the rinks at all. Whatever the reason, Quiet Moms are few and far between, but they do exist.

Quiet Mom is just as her title states. She is reserved and, if not unfriendly, still slightly unsociable. She usually drops off her player at the rink door and disappears until pick-up time. Even then, she stays in her car and waits for her young one to come to her. She knows exactly what's going on in and around the rink but will never let on that she does. The occasional Quiet Mom does come in, but she sneaks into the bleachers and sits alone, off to the side, tapping out messages on her phone as a signal to others that she's not free to chit-chat. If she does make eye contact, she'll nod her head to say hi, and the minute the game is over, she'll slink back to the safe haven of her car so she can avoid actually speaking to anyone. Who knows, she may be a silent assassin hired by a rival team to target our coach, or possibly a cunning woman who is still waiting for her chance to strike. Or maybe not. She's so reclusive, we will never know the truth about her.

Quiet Mom isn't a Super Clapper, a Leaner, or a Yodeller. She doesn't carry a team blanket or wear a Hockey Mom hoodie. She doesn't sit and gossip before games and she certainly never watches a practice. I can't say I blame her for that. She cheers internally. She never shows any sign of emotion or nerves during games and would never even dream of yelling at the ref. She is a nice, restrained lady, and you'll hardly ever hear a peep from her. When you really think about it, she is maybe the sanest Hockey Mom of us all.

Team Colours Mom

Here's to all you moms out there who are crafty enough to create pins, bracelets, sweaters, and scarves in your child's team colours.

As this mom proudly walks in to the rink, everyone from Mars to Venus knows what team she's supporting by the colours she's sporting. If she is seriously into crafts, she also makes these items available for sale to the non-crafty moms among us who like to wear a symbol of our team. She doesn't make any profit, of course. She just loves making things and sharing the Team Colours Mom spirit.

The chief tools of the Team Colours Mom are yarn, knitting needles, and crochet hooks. Some moms use beads to make pins or bracelets, but construction paper, scissors, and glue guns are reserved for use by the Team Colours

Mom whose kids are in the younger age divisions. One version of this mom makes signs and posters to tack up behind her team's bench or stick on hotel-room doors when the team is away at tournaments. As her player gets older, Team Colours Mom can't quite get away with making "Go Sweet Timmy" signs anymore, even though in her mind they are all about building team spirit, cheering on her player, and just making the team feel good. Team Colours Mom is the one who has a plastic horn to blow, a cow bell to clang, or pennies in a laundry detergent bottle to rattle madly at every goal, though you're more likely to see her with these props in girls' hockey than in boys'.

Another version of the Team Colours Mom is the Team Colours Blanket Mom. And I, again, am guilty of being this Hockey Mom. I do not knit or crochet blankets myself, but I always feel cold at the rink, and I don't like to sit through a game without something under my tush to keep me warm. So, on several occasions, I have purchased blankets done in my kids' team colours. I have also gone as far as embroidering my player's last name and number on these blankets. This is a bonus in disguise: if I accidentally leave a blanket somewhere, there's no question whose it is.

Goalie Mom

I am not a goalie's mom, so this chapter is based purely on observation, not personal experience. I am not sure I could handle being the mother of someone who is always either "a hero or a zero." This poor mom has to be a bundle of nerves – constantly. Which perhaps explains why they are often *so* very loud. I once heard a Goalie Mom say, "Girls, there isn't enough vodka in Russia for the mother of a goalie!" She might be right.

Everyone knows that goalies are typically a little different than the rest of the team. Well, their mothers are a little different in the Hockey Mom department too. The Goalie Mom normally spends the game pacing back and forth and can be known to "zone wander." At the end of each period, she will meander down the length of the rink to the zone that her goalie is now playing in, and resume pacing. If the game is close enough or if it's in overtime, the Goalie Mom may even go so far as to stray right out of the building. If she elects to stay inside, she *woos* and chirps as necessary, but she has the full potential to instantly mutate into Big Mouth Betty if anyone dares to go into the crease.

On rare occasions she'll undergo another transformation, something I have only ever seen happen to a Goalie Mom (though other moms may be vulnerable to this syndrome, under pressure). It's called the "I Swear I Don't Swear Syndrome" and it looks like this: As an already tense game gets even more stressful, the Goalie Mom, or G-Mom, as she's sometimes known, becomes increasingly loud and verbal. She'll start off saying, "I swear I don't swear . . . " and yet, every time the puck goes anywhere near the crease, she starts cursing in ways that would make an NHLer blush. She's usually very clever in her choice of swear words, throwing together combinations you've never ever thought of, followed, of course, by her trademark line: "Ladies, I swear I don't swear!"

OVERTIME

OVERTIME

Overtime is a phenomenon all of its own, and it brings
out the wildest, most intense Hockey Mom qualities.
I am probably the worst offender here. I have little or no
willpower to stay in control or exercise any type of restraint
when a game goes into overtime. My nerves get shredded.
Normally I stand, my face covered with my blanket. I'm
usually so preoccupied with my own ridiculous behaviour
that I don't watch what the other moms are doing. But
I have asked around, and people who have the stomach
to watch tell me that it is not unusual for most moms to
pace, to not even look at play and to just otherwise react
to the rest of the crowd's noise. The one thing about
overtime I can tell you for certain is that it's usually
when most of the moms in this book come to life in
loud, vivid harmony.

Well, ladies, I hope you've enjoyed yourselves reading this. I know I've had fun writing it.

No matter what type of Hockey Moms we are, we should take a few minutes to pat ourselves on the back for being such great ones. Crazy behaviour at the rink aside, we do the "hockey thing" for one reason. We love our kids. We choose to show it in different ways, but the message is the same. We will continue to spend our money on equipment, to spend our time driving to rinks, and to lose our voices cheering on our children. We will do what we do for the love of our kids and of the game. Hockey has given us great memories and relationships and has allowed each one of our hockey-mad children to learn how to compete and how to be a team player. I can't imagine what we'll do when our kids grow up and move out, but I have my fingers crossed that we'll become the next generation of Hockey Grandmoms and start a new chapter in the long story of our love for the game.